ALTERNATOR BOOKS™

BREAKTHROUGHS IN
SPACE TRAVEL

Wil Mara

Lerner Publications ◆ Minneapolis

Lerner Publications Company
A division of Lerner Publishing Group, Inc.
241 First Avenue North
Minneapolis, MN 55401 USA

For reading levels and more information, look up this title at www.lernerbooks.com.

Main body text set in Aptifer Sans LT Pro Regular 12/18.
Typeface provided by Linotype AG.

Library of Congress Cataloging-in-Publication Data

The Cataloging-in-Publication Data for *Breakthroughs in Space Travel* is on file at the
    Library of Congress.
ISBN 978-1-5415-3868-9 (lib. bdg.)
ISBN 978-1-5415-4374-4 (eb pdf)

Manufactured in the United States of America
1-45051-35878-7/12/2018

Contents

ONE SMALL STEP TOWARD MARS

Falcon Heavy lifts off in 2018. The rocket is 230 feet (70 m) tall.

In February 2018, thousands of people gathered in Florida to see the world's most powerful rocket launch. They cheered as a *Falcon Heavy* rocket lifted off in a cloud of smoke. It soared into the clear blue sky on top of a pillar of fire.

One of *Falcon Heavy*'s main jobs is to carry cargo into space. With twenty-seven engines powering the rocket, it can carry about 140,000 pounds (63,503 kg) of cargo. But the launch in February was the rocket's first, and *Falcon Heavy* didn't carry such a heavy load. Instead, it carried a cherry-red Tesla Roadster car.

SpaceX, the company behind *Falcon Heavy*, sent the car into space to draw attention to the launch. In the driver's seat was a dummy named Starman wearing a space suit. As the Tesla Roadster flew into the sky, the car's speakers played the song "Space Oddity" by David Bowie.

The car detached from the rocket and headed toward Mars, but it soon went off course and flew somewhere between Mars and Jupiter. Yet the launch was still a huge success. *Falcon Heavy* rockets could soon carry cargo to the International Space Station (ISS), the moon, and even help humans **colonize** Mars.

Starman and the Tesla Roadster could soar through space for millions of years.

CHAPTER 1

GETTING THERE AND BACK

Soviet technicians on the ground controlled *Vostok 1*'s flight into space.

The first craft to carry a human passenger to space was *Vostok 1*. It looked like a steel ball with a cone attached to one end and was about the size of a car. *Vostok 1* launched from the Soviet Union (a former group of republics including Russia) on April 12, 1961. Yuri Gagarin, a Soviet astronaut, was inside. The trip took Gagarin around Earth once and lasted less than two hours.

Spaceflight technology has advanced a lot since 1961. The governments of countries such as Russia and China regularly launch people into space to go to the ISS. Companies around the world are going to space too. Spacecraft launch with powerful rockets that break away from a **capsule** before they reach space. Most rockets fall to the ground, and they can't be used again.

Russian spacecraft such as this *Soyuz* vehicle bring international teams of astronauts to the ISS.

US astronaut Alvin Drew moves some storage containers on the ISS.

INSIDE A SPACE CAPSULE

A space capsule carries astronauts and everything they need to survive in space, including water and air to breathe. Temperature controls keep the astronauts warm. Lightweight materials help modern capsules weigh less and carry more gear than older capsules. Touch screen controls make them easier to operate.

Astronauts wear space suits for dangerous parts of their missions, such as during launch. The suits can protect astronauts if the capsule is damaged and loses its air. Modern suits are lighter than those worn on previous missions. They're also more flexible and made with material that allows water to escape while keeping air inside. This helps astronauts stay dry and comfortable. The suits' gloves have special finger pads that make it easy to use touch screens.

Space suits can provide warmth and air for astronauts in emergencies.

STEM FOCUS

The outside of a space capsule features lots of high-tech equipment too. Long sets of solar panels look like insect wings. The solar panels absorb sunlight to turn into electricity for the capsule. The outside of a capsule has high-definition cameras and **sensors**, antennas for communicating with people on Earth and the ISS, and a periscope to look around. The capsule has a compartment with a parachute to slow its descent when it lands on Earth.

CHAPTER 2

LIVING IN OUTER SPACE

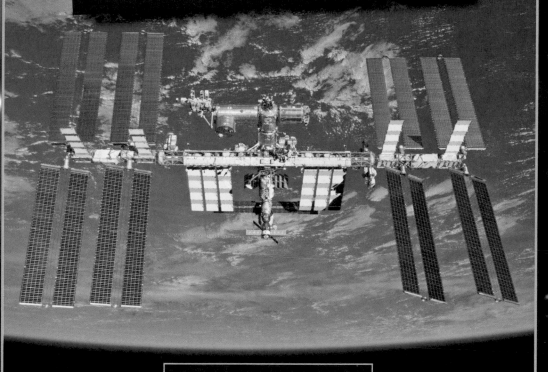

The ISS flies about 250 miles (402 km) above Earth's surface.

Modern astronauts spend more time than ever in space. They live on **satellites** such as the ISS. This high-tech research center, workplace, and laboratory **orbits** Earth and hosts astronauts from around the world.

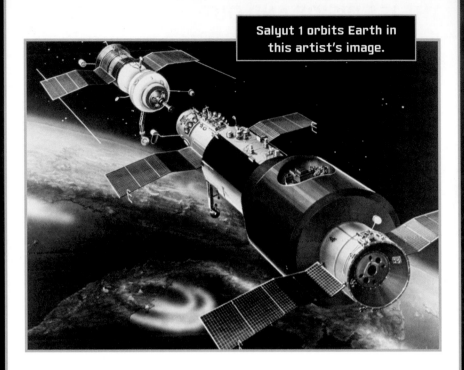

Salyut 1 orbits Earth in this artist's image.

THEN AND NOW

Several space stations have orbited Earth. The first—Salyut 1—launched in 1971 and stayed in space for less than a year. The ISS is the longest-orbiting space station. It reached space in November 1998.

The ISS consists of **modules**—sections that can be added or removed. Crew modules are for sleeping and eating. Science modules contain laboratories, research stations, and an observatory for viewing space. Other modules hold equipment for the systems that keep the ISS running, such as power and life-support systems.

THE ISS INSIDE AND OUT

The ISS is about as long as a football field and can comfortably hold six astronauts. With about the same amount of living space as a six-bedroom house, it has sleeping spaces, a gym, and windows that offer breathtaking views of Earth and space.

Koichi Wakata of the Japan Aerospace Exploration Agency looks out of a window on the ISS.

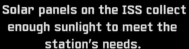
Solar panels on the ISS collect enough sunlight to meet the station's needs.

Modules and the gear they contain change depending on what experiments astronauts are running. Astronauts conduct experiments in physics, biology, and more. They may study the effects of space on the human body or see how the lack of **gravity** affects different materials. Often about 150 experiments run on the ISS at the same time.

The outside of the ISS has long solar panels to collect sunlight the station turns into electricity. About 8 miles (13 km) of wiring connect the station's electrical systems. They include more than fifty computers and about 350,000 sensors.

Sensors such as the Space Debris Sensor, which monitors small bits of material that strike the station, keep the ISS and astronauts safe.

The station has several docking ports where space capsules connect to the ISS. Capsules bring supplies and other important cargo from Earth, including new modules. The spacecraft also allow astronauts to come and go.

Astronauts Kimiya Yui (*left*) and Kjell Lindgren conducted many different experiments during a five-month trip to the ISS in 2015.

LIFE OF AN ASTRONAUT

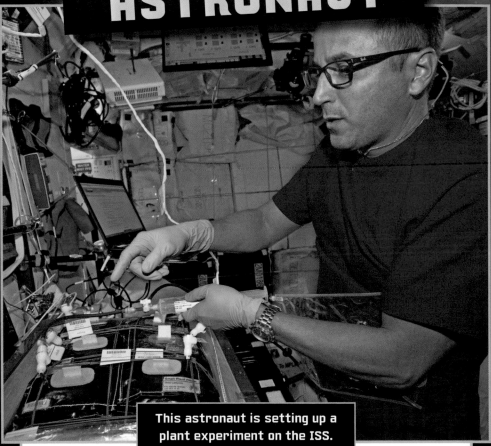

This astronaut is setting up a plant experiment on the ISS. Someday astronauts may be able to grow much of their own food.

Life in space is different from life on Earth in many ways. But it can be surprisingly similar too. Astronauts have everyday needs just like the rest of us.

EXERCISING

Astronauts work out to counter the effects of living without gravity. They usually exercise with special equipment for about two hours every day. The Advanced Resistive Exercise Device can strengthen muscles and bones without gravity. To use the device, astronauts push a bar up and down a set of tracks. A system of **pistons** provides resistance and makes the bar hard to push. Astronauts also work out on a treadmill. A harness keeps them from floating off the machine.

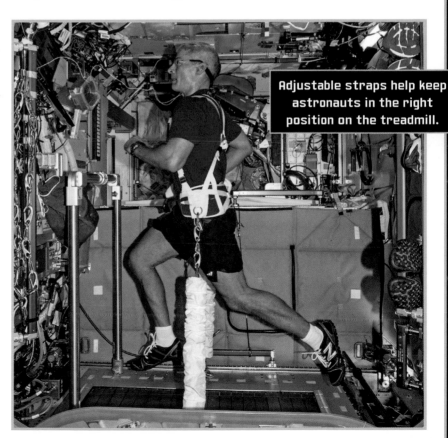

Adjustable straps help keep astronauts in the right position on the treadmill.

STEM FOCUS

Living without gravity might sound like a lot of fun, but it can lead to serious health issues such as weakened bones and loss of muscle tissue. As people move around on Earth, they use their muscles and bones to work against gravity. This keeps them strong. In space, astronauts don't use their muscles as much because they don't need to. Instead of walking across a module, they can just float. Astronauts may lose up to 5 percent of their muscle mass each week without exercise.

WASHING UP

To clean up, astronauts can't just step into a shower and turn on the water because the water would float away. Instead, they rub special soap and shampoo onto their bodies and hair. The soap and shampoo clean without water. Then astronauts use a damp washcloth or a sponge to wipe them off.

To prevent shampoo from floating away, astronauts squirt it directly into their hair and then spread it around.

MEALTIME

With no refrigerator on the ISS, food is stored in special ways. Many meals are freeze-dried—the water is removed from the food. Astronauts add water to these meals. Beef, chicken, and even pasta are prepared this way. Dry food such as nuts and brownies are also common in space. Drinks come in pouches with straws.

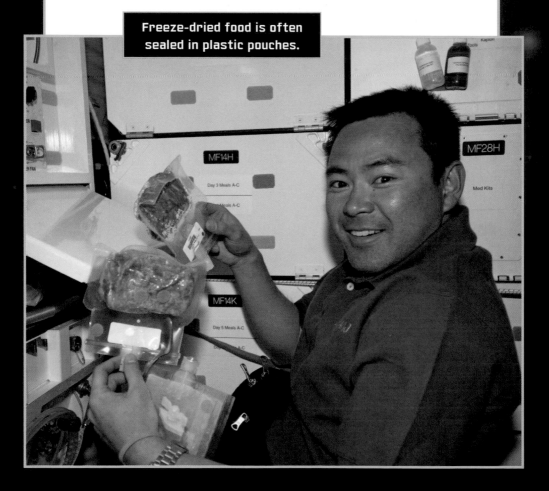

Freeze-dried food is often sealed in plastic pouches.

The ISS has an oven to heat and prepare meals. Sauces are available that will stick to food, such as ketchup and mustard. Dry goods such as salt and pepper could float away and may find their way into air vents, sensitive equipment, and the astronauts' eyes. Instead, astronauts have a liquid salt and pepper.

CHAPTER 4

LOOKING TO THE FUTURE

Some scientists believe life once existed and might even still exist on Mars.

Scientists are making exciting advancements in space travel. Space **probes** have explored Mars, comets, and the farthest reaches of the solar system. In 2012 the *Voyager 1* probe, which launched in 1977 to explore Jupiter and Saturn, became the first human-made device to leave the solar system. Spacecraft carrying people have landed on the moon but on no other natural space object. That might change in the near future.

TO MARS

In 2011 the National Aeronautics and Space Administration (NASA) announced it planned to develop a vehicle called *Orion* to take people farther into space than ever before. It would be part of a mission to explore Mars in the 2020s. In December 2014, NASA completed its first successful test flight of the *Orion* spacecraft—with no people aboard.

Astronauts would face many risks on a journey to Mars. It has taken about eight months for probes to get to the planet, so astronauts would be isolated from Earth for long periods. This can be hard on a person's mental health. Another danger is **radiation**. A **solar storm** may eject large amounts of radiation into space during the trip. Radiation can harm human cells and cause cancer and other health problems. NASA is working on solutions, such as shelters within *Orion* that astronauts could enter for protection against radiation during solar storms.

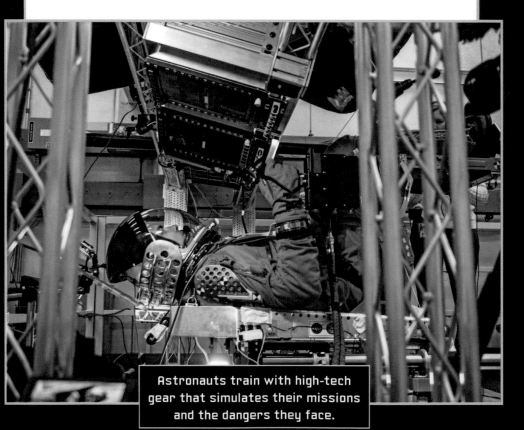

Astronauts train with high-tech gear that simulates their missions and the dangers they face.

SpaceX rockets demonstrate
their abilities in 2018.

PRIVATE SPACE TRAVEL

Billionaire Elon Musk started SpaceX to advance spaceflight and bring humans to other planets for the first time. The company's *Falcon 9* rocket has lifted capsules that brought supplies to the ISS. The *Falcon 9* can return to Earth and launch again, saving money and material. It and SpaceX's next rocket, the *Falcon Heavy*, can carry the *Dragon* capsule into space. The *Dragon* is designed to bring cargo to destinations in orbit and to carry astronauts and space tourists.

Amazon owner Jeff Bezos started a private space travel company, Blue Origin, in 2000. The company seeks to reduce the cost of space travel to allow more people to explore space. The company hopes that someday millions of people will live and work in space on stations and spacecraft. Other space travel companies, such as Virgin Galactic, are working toward similar goals.

Amazon is one of the world's most successful companies, giving Jeff Bezos plenty of money to pursue his space travel dreams.

Blue Origin is also designing rockets that it can reuse.

As humans travel farther into space, we learn more about our solar system and our place in the universe. Humans have walked on the moon, and soon people will travel to Mars. The journey will be dangerous, but astronauts—and the equipment they use—are up for the challenge.

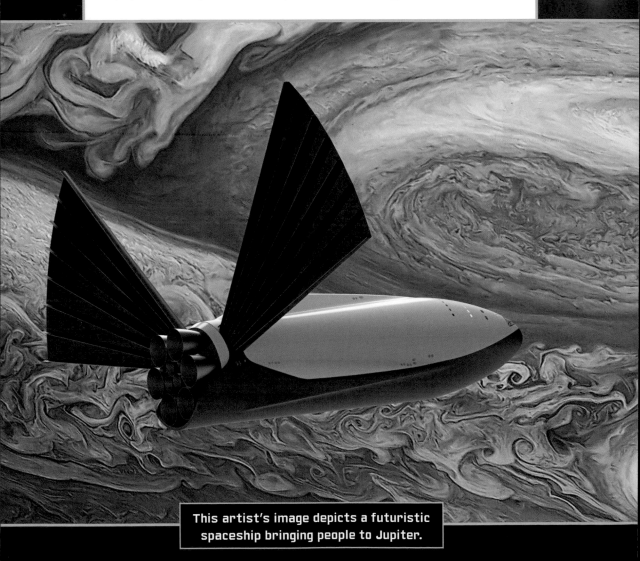

This artist's image depicts a futuristic spaceship bringing people to Jupiter.

One of the most exciting modern technology advancements is the 3D printer. It creates 3D objects by stacking layers of material on a platform. Modern 3D printers can make everything from toys to artificial limbs. Scientists are figuring out new ways to use 3D-printing technology in space travel. Someday astronauts may bring 3D printers to another planet. The printers could create useful things such as containers, solar panels, and even homes with materials astronauts find on the planet.

Astronaut Barry E. Wilmore holds a tool he made with a 3D printer.

capsule: a spacecraft designed to carry people and cargo

colonize: settle in a new place

gravity: the force that pulls things toward a planet or keeps objects in its orbit

modules: independent parts of a space vehicle or a space station

orbits: moves in a circle around an object in space

pistons: parts of a machine that slide up and down to move other parts

probes: tools or devices used to explore things, such as planets

radiation: waves of energy

satellites: objects that move around another body in space

sensors: devices that detect things such as light, heat, or physical impacts

solar storm: an event such as a solar flare that sends radiation from the sun into space

Beth, Georgia. *Discover Mars*. Minneapolis: Lerner Publications, 2019.

Easy Science for Kids: Space Travel
http://easyscienceforkids.com/all-about-space-travel/

Gitlin, Martin. *Personal Space Travel*. Ann Arbor, MI: Cherry Lake, 2018.

Goldstein, Margaret J. *Private Space Travel: A Space Discovery Guide*. Minneapolis: Lerner Publications, 2017.

NASA: For Students
https://www.nasa.gov/audience/forstudents/index.html

National Geographic Kids—History of Space Travel
https://kids.nationalgeographic.com/explore/space/history-of
-space-travel/#space-first-space-suit.jpg

Silverman, Buffy. *Mars Missions: A Space Discovery Guide*. Minneapolis: Lerner Publications, 2017.

SpaceX: Falcon Heavy
http://www.spacex.com/falcon-heavy

INDEX

Photo Acknowledgments

Image credits: SpaceX, pp. 4, 5, 25, 28; mechanick/Getty Images, p. 6; NASA/Joel Kowsky, p. 7; NASA, pp. 8, 10, 11, 13, 16, 19, 20, 21, 29; NASA/Robert Markowitz, p. 9; Sovfoto/UIG/Getty Images, p. 12; Thomas Pesquet/ESA/NASA, p. 14; NASA/ESA, pp. 15, 17, 18; NASA/JPL-Caltech, p. 22; NASA/Bill Ingalls, p. 23; NASA/Rad Sinyak, p. 24; Blue Origin, pp. 26, 27; Design elements: filo/Getty Images; Supphachai Salaeman/Shutterstock.com; satit sewtiw/Shutterstock.com.

Cover: Courtesy of SpaceX.